1. Introduction

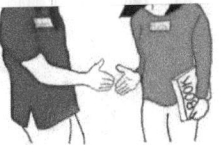

How many articles are there about making money online? Thousands? Millions? Enough? Probably. But there's a problem. Too many of them are just sales pitches to convince you to sign up for some seminar, webinar, training session or some other way to become an online millionaire.

They really give online money making a bad name. But it is possible to make money online. I mean, the people selling all of those millionaire pitches are making money, right?

There are legitimate ways to make money online. The problem is that the real ways to make money aren't "get rich quick" schemes.

Most of them require a lot of work and sometimes a lot of dedication before seeing a return on your time. But if you really want to make money online, work from home or turn an idea into a business, you *can* do it.

In this book , I'm going to tell you about all kinds of legitimate ways to make money online.

Ever since the idea of online auctions came into existence, the online selling market has been on the rise. Many are interested, but don't know how to get started. There are still all kinds of ways to make money by selling online, whether you're selling what you already have or buying and selling like a store. Before we get started, here are a few general tips when selling anything online:

Get a PayPal account. If you don't have a PayPal account, you'll want to get one if you're doing business online. It's the standard in online business for receiving payment and paying others.

Take good pictures. Some of the options below don't require you to actually take the picture and sell the product, but for the ones that do, make sure you take a clear picture that makes your product stand out from the others. If you're going to be taking a lot of pictures, set up a small "studio-like" area in your home with a backdrop and proper lighting to really make your pictures come across as professional. And of course, you'll want a good camera too.

Be honest. If you're selling used items, be honest about every dent, scratch, blemish, etc.. This will reduce many issues you could run into and keep your reviews positive.

Do good business. Plain and simple. Whether you're selling on a small site or opening an online store, your customer service matters. You'll want to get those positive reviews and make a good name for yourself. Respond to questions, concerns and complaints. Offer a guarantee if available.

Follow those guidelines and you will do well in online sales. When you're ready to start selling, here's where you go:

1. **Amazon** – Have you heard of FBA? It stands for "Fulfilled by Amazon" and it's getting pretty popular. Basically, you buy products (in bulk is best) and ship them to Amazon for them to store. When your products sell, Amazon packs them up, ships them out and sends you the money (after taking their cut). There are people making a full-time living from FBA, while others just do it for some extra money.

2. **CraigsList** – Some things don't ship very well. Other things may make you feel uncomfortable to sell to someone across the country. Anytime you're selling a large item or something you just don't want to ship, Craigslist is a great place to go. It's simple to list your item (again, take good pictures!). If you don't like the idea of putting your phone number out there, the interested individual can send you a message to your inbox without even getting your email address.

3. **eBay** – Of course you can't read an article about making money online that doesn't mention eBay. You can start an eBay store and get serious about it or you can just sell some stuff to declutter your home. Either way, I've made my fair share from selling on eBay and it's still a popular way to earn money. If you decide to start an actual eBay store, you'll want to find a drop-ship business like Doba that will store and ship items straight to your customers so you don't have to deal with an inventory.

4. **Etsy** – If you like to create arts and crafts, you can sell them on Dove puoi trovare di tutto da creativi di tutto il mondo's completely free to open an Etsy store. You simply sign up, post pictures of your creations and starting selling. You can choose your payment option, but PayPal is generally the easiest. Etsy makes it easy to sell and keep track of your

inventory. There is a small listing fee and they take 3.5% of every sale you make.

5. **Facebook** – Facebook swap shops are great for selling things locally. It's like CraigsList, but a little easier. You simply search for swap shops in your area and ask to join the group. Once you're in, take a picture of the item, write a quick description with the price and post it. It doesn't get much easier than that. You can generally expect to get about what you would get at a yard sale, maybe a little more.

3. Blogging

Hey look, a book about making money online that doesn't mention blogging. . . oh wait, here it is.

First off, I'm a blogger so it seems wrong not to mention it, but more importantly, it's a legitimate way to make money. It's quite possibly the least straight-forward way on this book, but it's very doable and it's also quite possibly the funnest way on this book. I love blogging and I know hundreds of bloggers who feel the same. So let's talk about making money blogging and what it really means.

Blogging is something that requires patience, persistence and discipline. It may mean writing everyday for over a year before you really start to see any money from it. There are exceptions to the rule, but from my dealings with other bloggers, it seems to be pretty common to spend one or even two years building your blog, your brand and your authority, before making any serious amount of money.

Some people argue that you can make money without a lot of traffic and while that is true in some circumstances, you will generally need a lot of website traffic to start earning from a blog and that takes a while. Once you've reached that point, here are the primary ways to monetize your blog and start earning:

1. **Advertising** – This is definitely the most old-school way of earning money with a blog. It's also starting to become the least common way. You can sell advertising spots directly on your site or you can sign up with a company like Google AdSense or Media.net. Either way, you won't see a whole lot of money from ads until your views are well into the thousands each day.

2. **Affiliates** – There are many affiliate networks, such as FlexOffers and CJ Affiliate that allow you to promote other people's products and services. You simply put a link or a banner on your page and then you get a percentage if someone clicks through and buys the product/service. You'll want to select products that are specifically within your blog's category.This is an effective way to earn money once you have the traffic coming to your blog.

3. **Membership** – Many people have created a paid membership area on their blog. This is typically for exclusive content that you can only access in the "member's area." If you have a really great idea on what to include, this can be a great idea. You'll have to create something that can't easily be accessed around the web.

4. **Products** – You can create your own product, such as an ebook or computer software. You would then use your blog as a promotion tool to get people to buy your product. As long as you create a legitimate product with a whole lot of value, you should be able to get some buyers, but like everything else with a blog, you'll need the traffic to get the sells.

5. **Services** – You can offer a paid service, such as life coaching, blog coaching, goal setting or financial planning. Just be sure to investigate all the legal implications and make sure you're not claiming to be a professional if you're not one. With a service like this, you're basically using your blog to sell yourself.

You'll need to convince people that you're worth buying and then be able to back up your claims once they purchase your service.

6. **Sponsored/paid posts** – Many blogs publish sponsored and paid posts. Sponsored posts are basically just posts about a specific brand, product or service. A company will pay you to publish an article about it. It's similar with other paid posts as well. Your basically selling the spot for the article on your site. If you decide to take this route, you'll want to build your traffic before you will get many offers.

7. **Subscription** – If you think of something valuable (newsletter, online magazine, etc.) that you can consistently offer on a certain basis (weekly, monthly, etc.), you may want to offer a subscription service. This could be a fee charged each time your product is sent out or on a monthly basis. Either way, this has to be something that your customers can only get by subscribing to your website.

8. **Videos** – This could be an entire section on it's own. Many people have made money by creating YouTube videos. Evan of EvanTube is a kid and he has made millions by creating reviews of products that other kids his age would use. It's not easy to get views into the millions, but once you do, you'll start seeing some cash come in. Many bloggers have completely turned to videos to get their point across by starting a video blog.

If you're truly interested in becoming a blogger, start by looking through the archives of ProBlogger, Copyblogger and Boost Blog Traffic. Then go read through all the free guides over at Quick Sprout. It may take you a year to complete those tasks alone, but it will be worth it. You'll practically have a MBA in blogging.

There are some companies that will hire you to work from the comfort of your own home. If you're interested in working for someone else, while still making your own schedule and deciding where to work from, here are a few companies that will let you do just that:

1. **CrowdSource** – CrowdSource offers many types of jobs from "microtask" jobs to larger writing and editing jobs. You decide how much you work and you can do most of it right at your computer.

2. **Demand Studios** – Demand Studios is hiring all kinds of creative professionals, from writer to filmmakers. The pay isn't amazing, but it's competitive for a work-at-home job.

3. **Fast Chart** – Fast Chart allows you to work from home as a medical transcriptionist. There are some requirments and qualifications listed on the page, but if you meet them, you'll make competitive pay for the

industry. You'll also be able to set your own schedule since you'll be working from home.

4. **Leap Force** – Leap Force is one way that Google rates websites for search engine ranking. If you're hired, you make decent money (usually over $11/hour), you set your own schedule and it can be pretty fun to view and rank websites.

5. **Liveops** – Liveops is a call center that allows you to work from home. Once your set up to take the calls, you can begin making a weekly schedule and working from home. The pay is generally close to $10/hour, but you can earn more with commissions.

6. **SpeakWrite** – SpeakWrite will pay you up to $15/hour to transcribe information. You set your own schedule and work from home.

Now you've got many different options to start earning online. If you saw something that really interests you, try it out and learn more about it. If you're really wanting to make a full-time income online, you need to be dedicated to learning how to do what you want to do. There are tons of free resources out there. You just have to search for them!

5. Bitcoin trading

Bitcoin is a cryptocurrency that is created by a pseudonym Satoshi Nakamoto. Invented on 31 October 2008, this digital currency was regulated in 2009 as an open-source platform.

Now talking about the Bitcoin trading, so let me tell you that bitcoin trading is profitable for professionals as well as beginners. There are plenty of benefits of trading Bitcoin such as –

1. **Bitcoin is Global**

Bitcoin is a digital currency that clearly means it is not related to economy of any country. Many countries like Japan and Australia have legalized Bitcoin as a payment method and demand of Bitcoin is increasing day by day.

2. **24/7 Trading**

As Bitcoin is a decentralized digital currency so there are no official Bitcoin exchanges unlike stock markets. It can be traded anytime across the world 24/7 and it will create the opportunity for exchanges too.

3. **Volatile**

Bitcoin is popular for its frequent price movements. Hence, this volatile factor of Bitcoin creates a lot of opportunities for traders.

4. Find Exchange

Miners or users need to consider many things before choosing Bitcoin exchange. The factors include location, fees, regulation and trust, and others.

However, if you want to start with cloud mining, there are many reliable Bitcoin cloud mining websites, including Hashgains, Genesis Mining, Hashing24 that can help you in mining Bitcoin easily and earn profits.

What is bitcoin trade?

The simplest way to think of this is to think of Bitcoin as anything else you'd have the capacity to buy with enough money. For example, one can buy a car/house/food with money.

Bitcoin was developed through technology that executes completely online. It is stored virtually, on wallets or exchanges. Everything is online and one can remotely transfer and send value to anyone online (stored in bitcoin as a currency). One can't touch their bitcoins the same way one can touch physical things such as a dollar bill, computer desk, a tree etc.

In short, Bitcoin is a virtual currency built by lines and lines of code (computer program). It's called a crypto currency because it's encrypted by code that can't be messed with.

So bitcoins can be "traded", i.e. bought and sold on an exchange. For example, if you have 50 USD and if you want to convert them to Euros, or any other currency what should you do? You'd go to a forex exchange service which will offer you the currency you're looking for, at a given exchange rate or fee for the transaction.

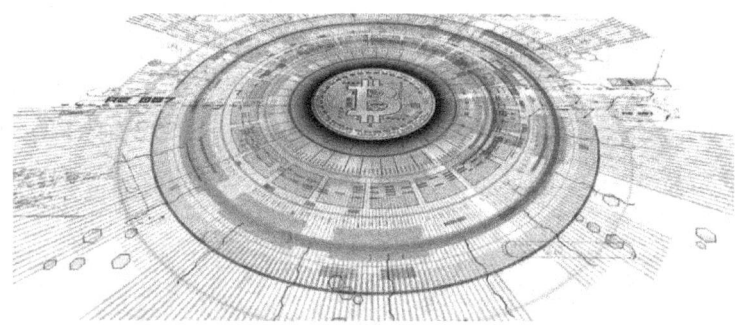

Similarly, one can buy bitcoin legally on cryptocurrency exchanges which are online. Most of the time, these exchanges are regulated by the government and one can buy these bitcoins using standard fiat money (money stored in a bank account).

"Bitcoin trade" is simply the buying and selling of bitcoin. These activities usually happen on cryptocurrency exchanges like Coinbase, Poloniex, etc.

6. Digital Marketing

Gone are the days where earning money was done through a traditional method of the day job. Now there are openings in the web to earn money through online. There are different ways available to earn money at this time and age.The latest buzz to earn money online is through digital marketing. Digital marketing is a great way to earn money online without being going out of the home.Well, now you must be wondering how to earn money by digital marketing. Before this one needs to understand the term digital marketing and proceed further to online money making with digital marketing.

Digital marketing is not the shortcut to earn money, like every other job we have to spend time and learn the basics of it before diving into it and then only you can find the ways to how to earn money in digital marketing. And, the more you learn and more you practice the digital marketing techniques, you can make considerable earnings from it.

What is Digital Marketing?

Digital marketing termed as an online platform where one can advertise their products online on the internet or any other digital medium. It's is the thing of the past, when salesman used to sell their wares by shouting their prices, attractions and their benefits in a community market. As people nowadays have a significant online presence, the sellers have grabbed the opportunity to create a niche for their product and this is where the concept of digital marketing comes in as it takes the details of the product to the customer anywhere and anytime as it uses social media and web pages to advertise the product.

There are various lucrative ways on how to earn money by digital marketing and some of the ways are listed below:

How to Earn Money by Digital Marketing?

There are certain number of ways by which one can earn money through digital marketing such as:

Content marketing

Blogging

SEO

Website designing

Social media marketing

Affiliate marketing

Mobile marketing

Email marketing

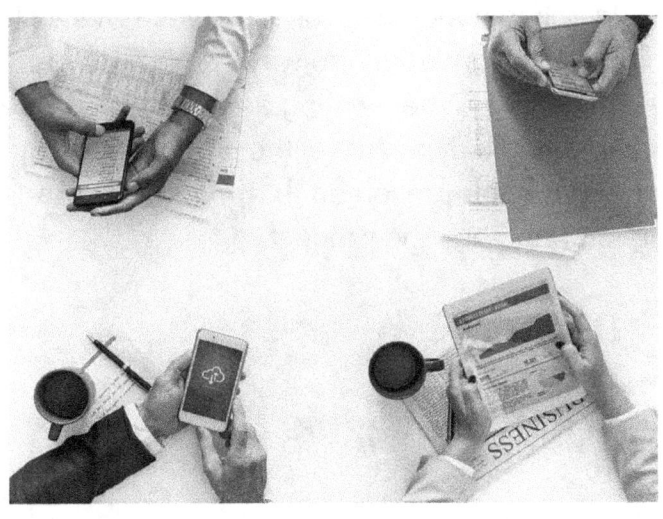

Content Marketing:

Content Marketing is termed as creating and publishing free content online with an intent to advertise a certain product or service. It is a bridge of information between the consumer and the seller. Content marketing is used in search engine searches. The current trend in buying now are;

Query searching- in the current trend people tend to search each and every issue on the internet.

Research- then comes the researching of many articles about the same subject and knowing their current market value, price etc

Comparison- then the consumer compares the different price quotes and decided the price suitable for them.

Buying- well here the end result the product is bought.

These steps are possible for online buying if there good search results to compare and buy if there is good content available online about the product. If you have a strong suit in writing then this is one of the ways on how to earn money by digital marketing. When writing a content you should be able to understand the dynamics of the product thoroughly and the content should be presented in a manner that a layman can understand and buy the product.

Blogging:

What is blogging?

Blogging is nothing but a personal opinion of the writer on any topic. There are a lot of blog sites which offer free hosting of opinions and it has the readability of millions of readers. If you are a creative writer then it is a rewarding job to write an appealing blog about the product and at the same time, online money making with digital marketing is achieved. But the basic requirement of the blog is that it should be always in current trend. You could also link Google Adsense and monetize your blog by hosting ads. For and each and every ad you hoist on your blog you will able to generate more income. In the blog, you can attract reader with steady and genuine content, offer a freebie in exchange for their email address, build their trust and then advertise a product on your blog which will really be useful to the reader and earn a commission if the readers use your blog as a link to purchase the product.

SEO (SEARCH ENGINE OPTIMIZATION):

Search engine optimization well it is a very big word but it is a very simple method of online money making once you get to know the specifics. The main aim of SEO is to increase your site's visibility in the search field. Every search engine gives a result based on certain keywords or key phrases of the search query typed in the box and the most relevant result gets to be on the top. Here comes the work of SEO professional who helps to optimize the website pages with the most searched keyword and key phrases to ensure maximum visibility of the website. You can earn money by building links or by writing SEO content which is written with the aim of attracting search engine traffic. you are required to write content with a rich mixture of keywords and phrases and improve the chances of the website being in the top suggested results. There are different types of SEO content writing like

Blog writing

Infographics

Videos

Slideshows

List making

Glossaries

Directories

Guides

Articles

Product pages

You can pick your niche and start earning in it, this is not a complete list but a comprehensive one there are many ways in this digital marketing methods to earn money.

Website Designing:

This area requires a certain technicality. If a person has the ability to design a website from scratch and maintain it in a way that is noticed by the user. Website design is a planning, structuring and creating and updating of the websites. It means the designer has to choose the correct specifics like an inviting layout, a splash of colors, the images used in them, creating a user-friendly interface for optimum navigation and presenting the website in a clutter free way. The designer should also keep in mind that the website has to be updated regularly to keep up with market trends. In this way of digital marketing, one can learn how to earn money by digital marketing from the comfort of home by designing websites according to the client's needs or restructure an existing website by giving it a makeover.

Affiliate Marketing:

This type of digital marketing is based on the weight of one's recommendations. Unlike other digital marketing ways, this affiliate marketing is based on one to one recommendations that are if you recommend a product to your friend and then he /she uses the link given by you to purchase the product then you would gain a commission out of that sale. This is called affiliate marketing. This is the oldest type of digital marketing. Many online e-commerce giants have successful affiliate marketing programs. It is also called referral marketing. In affiliate marketing, you can put a tie up with a company your referral link and this how to earn money by digital marketing to sell its goods through your referral link and earn commission for every product sold via your link.

Social Media Marketing:

Wondering how to earn money by digital marketing through social media:

As the name suggests it is a digital marketing which is done in the social media platforms like facebook, twitter, Instagram and other social media platforms. Nowadays a huge demographic use their free time to dabble in social media and chatting to like minded people. Most of the social media networks have their own data analytics tools which assist in building and advertising marketing campaigns in social media. As the there is a constant streaming of discussions and opinions in the social media there would be almost an immediate notice product and it would also be shared on other platforms leading to awareness about the product.

But this process is a little slow to catch up on, it is more of nurturing type of marketing. Social media marketing has a lot of unexplored potentials and a wide demographic to be explored. You could post a marketing campaign on your social media account and earn money for the number of campaigns posted in your account and a number of views you get from your friends and the success rate of your campaign will ensure you a profitable online money making with digital marketing. You could also share a post on social media on how to earn money by digital marketing to attract more views and use those view to advertise the product.

Mobile Marketing:

Mobile Marketing is an innovative way in digital marketing. It is a recently emerged trend for online money making with digital marketing. There are different ways of mobile marketing like:

- **SMS marketing** – this marketing is done by short messaging service or SMS. Before the emergence of the internet era, the products used to be advertised in this manner. Even now this method is used by small scale entrepreneurs.

- **Push notifications** – this was introduced by Apple in 2009 and this was replaced by google cloud messaging service later in 2013. Push notification is nothing but the message that pops on the mobile screen the viewer can see the message in a single tap.

- **App based marketing** – these are the recent trends in digital marketing. The developers help the product to gain maximum visibility in the app store. Mobile app development has become a lucrative way to earn money by digital marketing.

- **In game mobile marketing** – when playing an online game we see a lot of pop up ads in the game if you click on them they lead to the third party website urging the user to buy or download the app or game.

- **QR Codes** – these codes are scanned by the mobile camera and the URL is automatically entered in the browser's tab and the user can access the product easily without the hassle free site navigation.

Nowadays, almost everyone have a mobile phone. Hence, it can be a very rewarding way to earn money by digital marketing through mobile marketing, if the person has a very good niche of creative designing and making attractive captions in a few word. You can offer your services to create and send bulk SMS to a number of contacts which is a very viable option for local entrepreneurs to develop their business.

Email Marketing:

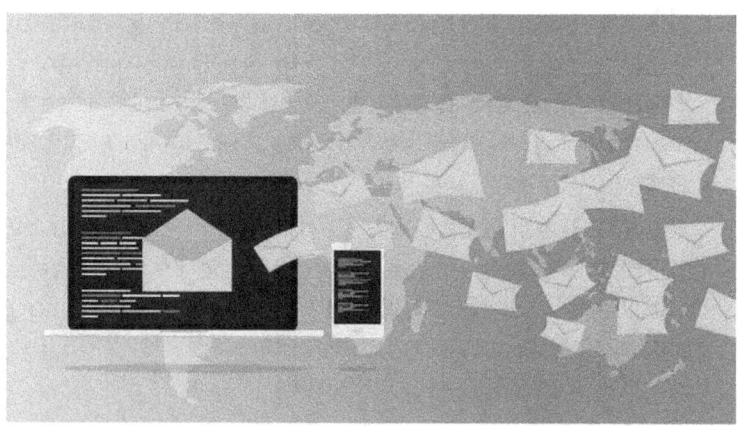

Email Marketing is an innovative way of marketing. It is a marketing tool in which an advertiser sends an email to the recipient detailing the products and the deals available in them. It has the potential to reach millions of customer in a single click. It is a mix of graphic content with contents and links which grant access to the customer for easy purchase and information. It is an easy way to gauge the customer's reaction and the marketing graph of the product. A lot of marketing emails come with the option of unsubscribing to eliminate unwanted customers and secure potential customers.

There also pre made templates in which the information can be filled and sent to the recipient without having the need to design or create a template. The pros of this type of digital marketing are the product is advertised to a large audience and it has a far outreach than the traditional method of marketing. The cons of this method are sometimes when a person gets a bunch of marketing emails they tend to dismiss them without a single glance. So it is highly important that the email marketing created is very attractive and creative in a single glance. But the important part of this system is your mailing list. It is not about how long it is about how many leads you have in it which are definite winners. Now there are email marketing campaigns that pay you when the lead clicks on the link provided in the email. Now that's another way on how to earn money from digital marketing.

How To Make Money Using Udemy and Online Course Marketplaces

What Do You Need To Get Started?

All you need to get started are these few items…

1) Computer/Laptop – I use a Macbook Pro (I know they're not cheap but they're definitely worth the investment)

2) A decent microphone – you don't have to be some super master sound engineer and go overboard here. The mic I use is a **Blue Yeti USB microphone** that you can pick up on Amazon for about $100. *I also recommend picking up an* *inexpensive pop filter to block out additional noise. I purchased a black Whisperteknik foam windscreen which you can also find on Amazon.*

3) Screen recording software – I have a Mac and highly recommend ScreenFlow, but if you are using a PC, I recommend Camtasia. *Both of these softwares are extremely simple and intuitive to use. Don't worry, you don't need a Masters degree in video editing and motion graphics to whip out high quality videos with these tools.*

In any case **Udemy has plenty of inexpensive online courses**
if you want to take your Video Production up a level.

In addition to the above, I recommend recording in a quiet place so you don't get much noise or feedback. Good audio is a high priority to many of the course marketplaces.

TIP #1: Like I mentioned, you DO NOT already have to be an "expert" or what you consider to be the absolute top authority in your niche to be good at this or to have success. The majority of courses I published were just my spin on content of courses that I had just bought and consumed. You probably already know a lot about more about a certain topic than most people, but if you're absolutely drawing a blank when coming up with ideas for content to teach, just get a subscription to Lynda.com – it's only like $25/mo. Go through a couple courses that interest you, and teach those things you just learned. I guarantee if you do this you'll absolutely make at back least the cost of your subscription within your first 30 days or less IF you take action.

TIP #2: Also, if you're worried about being on camera or you don't like your voice – you gotta just push past that fear and get over it. When I started out I sucked too, but I got better and improved over time. However, even to this day I still cut out all my ahhhs and umms – I almost never record it perfect on the first try.

TIP #3: If you're concerned about not being "expert enough" for people to buy from you, do not let this stop you from taking action. If you have some awesome credentials, great, you can use them in places like your profile or biography for these platforms. But if not, that's fine too, just be honest. But also be creative with it and try and squeeze out as many strengths and accomplishments that you've achieved in your life, because your profile is really your opportunity to brag about all the things you've done and shine...kind of like the cover letter of a resume. The most important thing is that people want to buy from others they like, trust and that are just real and genuine and know what they're talking about. And even though you may not consider yourself the tippy top "expert" in your entire niche yet, for the person who knows absolutely nothing about what you're creating a course around, you're a little more expert than they are. So, again, don't let that fear stop you.

Learn. Do. Teach.

– Go learn something

– Do it, so that you know what you're talking about and can speak from experience when you're teaching

– And then teach what you just learned to others

It's really that simple.

Create A Course Outline

To do this think of what you want to teach, and then figure out how you can break that down into simple steps. Each step will be a separate lecture or video.

I should try and make most courses about an hour or so. Now, that may seem like a long time. But to make it really easy for myself, I break each step into short videos.

If you were to teach something that included 12 steps and you needed to have one hour of content, that would mean only talking for 5 minutes about each step, which anyone can do.

Then, when you're done, you just assemble all the pieces, and now you have a full hour long course.

What Are Some Of The Most Popular Course Platforms?

Udemy
– this is basically the Google of the online course marketplaces. It's the largest and most popular.

Skillshare – my recommended place to start out because they let you upload individual lessons. Each lecture only has to be a minimum of at least 10 minutes. This platform will be the easiest and fastest to scale since there's no course approval process, and will put some quick money in your pocket.

StackSkills – this is another large platform that has a wide reach and can promote your courses out to their massive audience for exposure. They do like to promote courses as bundles, so you'll need to have a few courses complete and put together before you reach out to them.

ULearning – this is a newer platform. It's very similar to Udemy and makes it easy to upload and publish content, but I'm not 100% on how well this one will do, since at the time of me writing this they just recently launched.

Amazing – this is also a newer platform launched by Matt Clark, one of the people behind the massively successful Amazing Selling Machine. This is a unique platform and kind of a hybrid between Skillshare and Udemy. Worth checking out because I believe there will be greater chance to earn more revenue on this platform than other marketplaces, but it might be helpful to get your feet wet at somewhere like Skillshare or Udemy first.

How do I get good reviews for my courses?

On many of these platforms you do have the opportunity for students to leave reviews. We all know the power of reviews due to sites like Amazon. Reviews are extremely powerful and provide social proof that helps in driving more sales and profits. But to get good reviews don't overthink things. Number one, focus on creating the highest quality and valuable content that you can on your topic. Then next you can prompt students at various points throughout the course to take action and leave a positive review or rating if they have enjoyed the content inside, to help encourage others to enroll. You can also incentivize them in some way in exchange for a review, like sending them a content upgrade or free report, video or interview. That's really all I've ever done. *Keep it simple.*

When do I get paid?

Each of the platforms are different in how you get paid, when you get paid and what you get paid for. But most typically pay out a full calendar month after the current month.

For instance, if you earned $1000 in August, you would typically be paid out during the first week of October. But some pay on the 1st and 15th or later in the month. The most important thing for beginners is to just get started. Once you start getting results then you can begin planning out your months in order to reach your financial goals. Like if you wanted to reach a certain income goal by March, well you really need to be hustling hard in January because March is going to be the payout month of January's efforts and activity.

How much of a cut (%) does the online course marketplace take?

This varies, depending on the company. But lets look at Udemy as an example. There is a good number of options available depending on how the customer found the course. (via an Affiliate, via Udemy or directly via the Instructors promotion)

For example if a student purchases your course using an Instructor Coupon code, either from promotions to your own audience (e.g., your email list or YouTube subscribers) you can make 97% revenue share. Alternatively if the course is sold via an Affiliate, the split is 50% affiliate, 25% Instructor and 25% Udemy. If the sale comes directly via the Udemy website (not an affiliate or an instructor promotion) the split is 50% Udemy, 50% Instructor.

You can make a lot of money with Udemy but like everything in life – the more effort, the more rewards!

97% is very generous – but you have to find the customer. I have been happy for Udemy to do the selling, marketing and driving traffic – which in most instances means 50% revenue share.

8. Join Paid to click sites

What are Paid to click sites?

Paid to click sites, simply called as PTC, a business model that offers instant real human traffic to a website or blog or business and in turn they will pay a small penny of the amount to those visitors for visit these sites.

How can you work?

Register a free account. Make a habit to log in daily and view all available ads in their advertisement page.

You will be paid just for watching ads like you are watching advertisements on TV.

How much can you make?

You will be paid between $0.0001 to $0.01 depending on the length of the advertisement you are watching.

All your payments will be made to your Bank account via the online processor such as PayPal or Payza.

So you need to open an account with those processors to get your payment. Join many sites and work simultaneously to get more income.

This method does not require any investment to start but you can earn money for sure.

If you are well at writing based on a certain topic then there are greater chances to make money from your skill.

80 out of 100 bloggers are searching for content writers to write contents for their blogs and there is always 80 chances out there when a new 100 blog launched.

Before writing articles you must pose certain qualification to write for a blog or website.

Learn On-Page SEO for writing articles before writing. You can get anywhere from Rs.100 to Rs.500 per SEO friendly quality article.

Write deep lengthy articles of more than 1500Words so that you can get more pay. Do not worry who will buy your articles?

There are many websites out there whose prime business is selling articles for bloggers. Article writers like you should open a free account there and complete your profiles.

Register your account with article base, Article biz, Ezine articles etc.

Submit your article in the right category. They will display your article for sale and on the successful sale, you will be paid. You can easily earn Rs. 5000 weekly without putting much effort.

Make a habit of writing at least 1 article per day. If you paid Rs.250 per article per day you can get Rs.7500 per month.

Spend at least 1 – 2 hrs to write articles will make you earn decent income every month.

A VALUABLE E-BOOK IS A POWERFUL SIGN-UP INCENTIVE FOR NEW SUBSCRIBERS

Does your email list grow s-l-o-w-l-y, with perhaps one or two new subscribers each week … at best?

The truth is that readers are reluctant to hand over their email addresses – even if they love your content. So they may need a little extra nudge to sign up (you could even call it a bribe).

An e-book packed full of valuable content makes a great incentive. If you can offer free information your audience

41

would gladly pay for, you'll see dramatic improvements in your sign-up rates.

AN AUTHORITATIVE E-BOOK POSITIONS YOU AS AN EXPERT IN YOUR FIELD

If you want to build a name for yourself in your field, an e-book is a great way to boost your credibility and authority.

By publishing on Amazon, you can appear literally alongside some of the biggest names in your industry.

In fact, you may find you get *more* reviews and attention than much better-known authors who are simply less web-savvy.

Why Most E-books Are Embarrassingly Bad

On the surface, writing an e-book seems relatively easy.

Lots of bloggers seem to be doing it, so how hard can it be?

But in reality, most e-books that see the light of day are horrible. Embarrassingly bad.

That's because your average e-book author doesn't have a clue about writing a book. And they don't have any of the support that a traditional author would be given by their publisher.

But producing a quality e-book is almost as hard as publishing a traditional book. The basic tasks are the same. It's just that you have to do them all yourself.

Which is why avoiding the mistakes that catch most first-time e-book authors is critically important.

Planning Mistakes: How to Doom Your E-book Before You Even Start Writing

Even before you start writing your e-book, you can make some crippling mistakes. I had two spectacular e-book flops due to the second mistake on this list, and many of the others have cost me valuable time.

So avoid the following dumb mistakes if you don't want to fall at the first hurdle.

CHOOSING A TOPIC YOU KNOW LITTLE ABOUT

If you want to create a premium e-book , you can be tempted to pick a "hot topic" thinking that's where the money is.

Likewise, when creating a sign-up bribe, you might think you need to entice readers with the latest information about an emerging topic.

And if you're publishing on Amazon, it's easy to think you need to target one of the most popular categories.

But picking a topic like this is a BIG mistake.

If you know little or nothing about your chosen topic, creating an e-book will be a huge amount of work. You'll have to do a ton of research, interview experts, and perhaps even pay a real guru to get you up to speed.

How to Fix It

Write about something you actually know about – which almost certainly means tying your e-book to your blog's core topic. **You'll not only save a ton of time on research, you'll also have a ready-made audience for your writing.**

WRITING THE E-BOOK YOUR AUDIENCE "NEEDS"

I've fallen into this trap myself (twice) and I've seen a heck of a lot of other bloggers do the same.

It happens when you realize there's a topic you know your readers *need***, and you know you can write the perfect book that will genuinely help them.**

Sounds great, but people don't always know what they need. And your sense of what it is might not be spot-on either.

How to Fix It

Don't give your readers what you think they need. Give them what they know they want.

How? Run a survey, and ask your readers to choose between three or four e-book topics.

(This is also a good opportunity to find out how much they'd pay, whether they're beginners or more experienced, and what specific questions they need your help to answer.)

THINKING LIKE A WRITER, NOT A PUBLISHER

Planning isn't just about deciding what you're going to write and what order you're going to write it in.

Because when you decide to create an e-book, you're not just a writer; you're also a publisher (and marketer).

If you don't start thinking *now* about how you'll sell your book – whether that means selling it for money or just selling the concept to your readers – you'll run into problems later on.

How to Fix It

Draft your sales page while you're planning your e-book. Make it sound as attractive and useful as and use that pitch to drive the writing process. This will make your e-book much stronger, *and* will make your life much easier when you launch it.

PICKING UP YOUR PEN (OR LAPTOP) AND STARTING TO WRITE

Once your survey results are in, you might be tempted to start writing straight away.

Whoa there.

Jumping into the writing at this point will cause you serious problems within days. You'll find yourself repeating things, or wasting time exploring ultimately unhelpful tangents.

How to Fix It

Plan your e-book before you start writing.

This means having a clear outline that has, at the very least, a title for each chapter. Yes, that might seem a bit boring, but it will make the writing stage far easier (and more fun).

This doesn't have to mean opening a blank document and writing a linear outline. Try freeform brainstorming or mind maps or index cards as creative alternatives to help get your ideas flowing.

TRYING TO MAKE YOUR E-BOOK TOO VALUABLE

With your first e-book, it's easy to think you need to deliver *the* definitive e-book – the only one your audience will ever need.

If that sounds like a good plan, ask yourself this: *"What will I give them next?"*

Chances are, you won't write just one e-book. You might write several in the same series, or you might create a short starter e-book for free, and then write a more advanced one to sell.

Even if your e-book is destined to be your subscriber incentive, if you give your readers everything they'll ever need, why would they come back to your blog?

How to Fix It

Go back to your survey and determine what aspects your audience cares about the most. Focus on those. If you have lots of extra ideas, great! Keep them in a separate place and use them for your next e-book. Or explore them in a detailed blog post.

If you inadvertently miss something crucial, you'll find out when you get feedback, and you can add a new section or chapter to address that point.

Writing Mistakes: How to Waste Time, Lose Focus and Give Up

Some bloggers love the *writing* part of creating an e-book; others find it hard going.

But whatever your feelings about writing, the follow mistakes can seriously curtail your progress … and may even make you give up altogether.

STARTING AT THE BEGINNING

Although it might be the first chapter in your book, your introduction almost certainly *isn't* the place to start writing.

It's hard to know what to include until you've drafted the majority of your book, and you don't want to get bogged down at this early stage.

If you start with the introduction, you'll often end up writing far more than you need to. And let's be honest. No reader relishes the sight of a long introduction – they want to dive into the real content.

How to Fix It

Don't begin with the introduction; start with your first "proper" chapter. Once you've drafted the rest of your book, you'll know what needs to go in the introduction.

Also, a lot of "introductory" material can go at the back of the book – I strongly recommend having an *About the Author* page at the back, because it's a great opportunity to point readers to your website, mailing list, and so on.

ONLY WRITING WHEN YOU FEEL LIKE IT

Although your e-book is probably a high-priority project for you, it can be genuinely tough to carve out the time for working on it regularly.

But if you don't write consistently, you'll never build up any momentum. You may write for a few hours to begin with, but then end up taking weeks off … and never getting back to your e-book.

How to Fix It

You don't have to write thousands of words at a time. One of my clients wrote a short chapter every week, without fail, and finished her e-book within a few months.

Find a consistent time each day, or several times a week, to work on your e-book. You might like to try the Pomodoro technique (25 minutes writing, 5 minute break) to use your time effectively during short writing sessions. Anyone can write for just 25 minutes.

If you know you have a problem with time management, address that now; it'll pay off for years to come.

LETTING YOUR INNER EDITOR TAKE THE LEAD

If you're writing regularly and staying focused but making slow progress, then you're probably trying to edit *while* you write.

Perhaps you find yourself typing a couple of paragraphs, then changing your mind and deleting them. You might even be stopping every sentence or two to make minor tweaks.

This is a serious drain on your productivity as a writer.

How to Fix It

If you change your mind about a whole paragraph or section, leave it in as is, but jot a note to yourself about it. You may find, on re-reading, that it works perfectly well.

QUITTING JUST BEFORE IT GETS EASY

After you've been working on your e-book for weeks, perhaps months, you may find that you've not made the progress you'd hoped for.

Whatever the exact cause (illness, workload, etc.), you've hit a wall. You aren't even halfway through the draft, and there's a long way to go.

When you go through a patch like this, it's quite tempting to just give up – to cut your losses, and leave that e-book draft abandoned on your computer.

But that would be a huge mistake. Because this is often a sign that things are about to get easier.

How to Fix It

Push yourself to reach the halfway point. Once you're halfway, natural momentum kicks in, and you'll speed up as you approach the end.

Be sure to remind yourself of your motivation for starting the e-book in the first place: what's it going to do for you and your blog? How will it help your readers – the people who you've come to know and care about?

Editing Mistakes: How to Wreck a Good First Draft

Although you probably won't spend as much time editing as you spent writing, this is the point at which your e-book really takes shape.

Editing makes the difference between a book that's simply "okay" and a book that's a well-polished, professional representation of you at your best.

The following mistakes will keep your e-book from becoming the masterpiece it deserves to be.

TRYING TO KEEP UP THE MOMENTUM

While it's important to not let your e-book stall after the first draft, you don't need to rush into editing. Some writers dive straight into the editing phase – but then they struggle to get perspective, and may quickly feel burned out.

How to Fix It

Let your e-book "sit" for at least a couple of days (and preferably a full week) before you begin reviewing and editing. That way, you'll come to it with fresh eyes and a new perspective – you'll be able to see what's already good, and what needs a bit more work.

With a little distance, you'll be able to see your work from the perspective of a reader, not a writer.

THROWING YOUR BEST WORK IN THE FIRE

Many e-book authors start their edit using the same file they used for the draft – for example, MyEbook.doc.

While that's not always a problem, it's seriously frustrating if you cut something you later want to put back in.

Worse, if you manage to delete, lose, or somehow corrupt that master file, all your hard work could be gone for good.

How to Fix It

For each new draft, create a new version of your file – MyEbookV2.doc, MyEbookV3.doc and so on. And create regular backups. A simple way is to email yourself a copy of the latest version from time to time.

REVIEWING WITH A MICROSCOPE, NOT A TELESCOPE

If you start your editing by looking for minor typos, you'll miss much more significant issues.

By focusing on the micro detail, you may fail to address major problems with your book – like "Chapter 15 is way too short" or "Chapter 7 should come after Chapter 10." These often require a bit of perspective.

How to Fix It

Read through your whole e-book, preferably in .pdf form, on paper, or on your tablet, before you begin editing.

In other words, read it in a format where you can't easily make small changes as you go along to force yourself to concentrate on the bigger picture.

Make a note of any issues you need to fix, like chapters in the wrong order, repetitive information, tangents that need deleting, and new sections you want to add.

TELLING YOURSELF YOU DON'T NEED AN EDITOR

When you've been working away on your own for (probably) several months, seeing mistakes can be tough – from the big picture issues to the small details like missing words or misplaced apostrophes.

But many first-time e-book authors are either too inexperienced to know the value of an editor or figure it's a luxury they can't afford.

Even if you're not in a position to pay for a full edit, that doesn't mean you have to go it alone.

How to Fix It

Consider paying for an editor to review just the first few chapters of your e-book. Many problems the editor identifies will probably occur throughout the e-book and you can fix them yourself once you know what to look for.

Recruit volunteers to help edit: ask your readers, or members of any blogging community you belong to. Be prepared to repay the favor!

HIRING THE WORLD'S WORST PROOFREADER

Once you've made any major changes and addressed the suggestions of your editors, your book is *almost* complete.

But before it's ready to publish, you'll need to do at least one complete read-through to catch any remaining typos or errors.

However, you're probably the worst person to catch those errors.

You've likely become so familiar with the content and its layout that you'll miss typos that will be obvious to someone else.

How to Fix It

If you can afford a professional proofreader, or if you have a talented friend who can help out, brilliant.

If you have to do most or all of your proofreading alone, here's the secret: don't proofread your e-book in the same environment that you wrote it. Try changing the font style and size and printing it out, or reading it on a tablet. You'll be surprised at how errors stand out.

INDULGING YOUR INNER PERFECTIONIST AND PROCRASTINATOR

Quality matters, but if you're onto your fifth proofread and you're spending ten minutes debating whether or not a particular sentence needs a comma, you're wasting time.

Even books from major publishing houses have mistakes from time to time. You may never have noticed this, because (like every reader) you don't pause and scrutinize every word.

How to Fix It

Give yourself a deadline for finishing the editing phase, and accept that catching 99 percent of your mistakes is good enough.

Don't agonize over the possibility that a typo may still be present. Readers aren't likely to notice, and if someone *does* point out a particularly glaring mistake after publication, it's simple to update your e-book.

Publishing Mistakes: How to Make Sure Your E-book's an Instant Flop

You could create a water-tight plan, write a hugely valuable e-book, and edit it till it shines, yet if you mess up its publication, you won't get the results you deserve.

But if you avoid the following mistakes, you'll give yourself the best possible chance of e-book success.

ASSUMING YOU KNOW THE BEST FORMAT FOR YOUR E-BOOK ALREADY

Even if you started out with a specific end goal in mind, be sure to review your options once you've finished your e-book.

An e-book that started life as a subscriber incentive might in fact make a great premium product, or serve as an authority-building book in the Kindle Store.

But if you don't at least consider other options, you might miss out on a huge opportunity.

How to Fix It

Depending on the final destination of your e-book, a range of different publishing options are available to consider:

If you're giving your e-book away as an incentive for joining your email list, then .pdf-only is simple and straightforward.

If you're positioning your e-book as a premium product (e.g., at least $10), you can just create a .pdf ... but you might also want to offer .epub and .mobi formats. You could also include multimedia bonus material on a password-protected webpage (e.g. audio interviews, short video tutorials).

If you're publishing your e-book on major retailers' sites, you'll need a lower price (usually $9.99 or less) and to publish your file in the appropriate format for the store.

And don't assume that a particular option is right for your e-book just because it's what you've seen other bloggers doing.

USING THE FIRST (YAWN-INDUCING) TITLE THAT COMES TO MIND

Just like a blog post title, an e-book title must grab attention. It's going to be the first (and quite possibly the only) thing your potential e-book reader sees.

How to Fix It

If you've had a working title in mind since the planning stage, now's the time to figure out whether it's truly good enough. You might want to ask your blog readers to vote on different titles, to find out which is the most compelling.

The same goes for the headline on your sales page — you'll probably want to put something a bit more intriguing than just the title of your e-book.

DESIGNING YOUR OWN FRONT COVER

Like it or not, everyone judges books by their covers.

Unless you're a professional designer, creating your own cover is a hugely damaging mistake.

Your e-book will look amateurish, and readers may well be put off from buying it.

This is especially true if you'll be selling your e-book on Amazon (or other e-retailers' sites) where most potential readers won't have any prior knowledge of you.

For plenty of examples of both good and bad covers, take a look at Joel Friedlander's Monthly e-Book Cover Design Awards.

How to Fix It

If you can afford it, hire a designer. This is a crucial investment, and you'll likely sell enough extra copies to more than pay for the designer's work.

But if you really have to create your cover yourself, keep it simple and straightforward, and look at *lots* of examples of good and bad designs.

FORGETTING TO LINK BACK TO YOUR BLOG

Your e-book might be a reader's first contact with you (if they bought it from Amazon for example). And even those who downloaded your e-book from your blog might forget where they got it.

So failing to link your e-book back to your blog is a big mistake. You're missing an opportunity to drive new subscribers to your main email list or to a separate list that tells your current e-book readers about your next book.

How to Fix It

Include a page at the back of your e-book – after "About the Author" – that lets readers know where to find you online.

Be sure to link to your subscriber landing page, to your next book's sales page, or anywhere else online you want to send them – e.g., your social media profiles.

Also important is giving your readers an easy way to send you feedback for your book, such as a dedicated email address or a link to a contact page.

And don't be afraid to link to relevant blog content within the body of the e-book itself.

COMPLETELY IGNORING THE POWER OF SOCIAL PROOF

Even if a reader already knows you, they won't necessarily trust that your e-book is any good until it has at least one review or testimonial.

Whether your e-book is available for purchase or simply a reward for new subscribers, people probably won't trust its value unless they can see that other people have read it and found it useful.

And if you're in a niche that's known for having a few sleazy operators, or one where e-books are rare, then failing to provide social proof is an even bigger mistake.

How to Fix It

Be proactive — send out review copies to bloggers in your niche, and to any of your blog's readers who've commented regularly or emailed you recently. Add positive reviews to your sales page and, if possible, use photos of the reviewers to boost credibility.

And if you can, send out your review copies *before* you launch your e-book – preferably at least a couple weeks before. This gives people a chance to read your book and get a review ready on or soon after your launch day.

ACTING LIKE YOUR E-BOOK ISN'T A BIG DEAL

Many bloggers are uncomfortable marketing their e-books so their "launch" simply involves a new link on their blog and a couple of low-key posts on social media.

But even the best e-book will wither and die without some determined promotion.

And the truth is that if you're not willing to market your e-book when the hard work of writing it is complete, you've basically wasted all that time and effort.

How to Fix It

You're proud of your new e-book, right? So start acting like it. (If you don't feel a swell of pride about your work then go back to the writing and editing phases until you do!)

Despite any preconceptions, you can effectively market your blog without coming across like a used car salesman.

Here's how…

Mix up your promotional messages with lots of useful and interesting content.

If you're giving people useful information at the same time as promoting your e-book, you'll feel less like a pushy salesperson.

If your e-book is on Amazon, you can create some buzz by giving it away free for short periods.

If this is your first premium product, make sure you tell your existing list about it and consider offering a discount for existing subscribers.

Write guest posts for popular blogs in your niche, and direct readers to a dedicated landing page for sign-ups or for the sales page for your e-book.

You might even look into ways to do something more interesting and innovative, maybe creating videos, offering special extras, or getting readers involved.

When Will You Make The Leap From Blogger to Author?

Lots of mistakes are lurking out there to trip you up on the path to publishing your first e-book, but the potential rewards are great.

You can get more subscribers for your blog, more authority in your niche and even earn more money from your writing.

And now that you know the most common mistakes, you can avoid them with ease.

But of all the mistakes you can make, one trumps them all.

Not even trying.

Or telling yourself that you'll write your e-book *someday*.

But you're not going to make that mistake, right?

So grab your calendar, take a look at the next week, and choose a day to begin.

Because in just a month or two, you could easily have a finished e-book … one that could supercharge your email list, position you as an expert, or start bringing in a steady income.

When will your e-book journey begin?

YOUR COUNTDOWN HAS BEGUN

And there are many more ways you can find on internet to make money online which I may have missed in this book (I am not perfect !) . Now you have NO reason not to get off your butt and DO something.

Get moving. You see, there is now a "countdown" running that you

weren't aware of. Now that you've completed this final chapter, the

clock has started ticking.

Here's the thing: if you don't take some sort of small action

towards the Online Earning within twenty-four hours, I believe it's almost guaranteed that you will never take ANY action towards your Online Earning.

With every passing second that you don't take action, this book

comes closer and closer to becoming yet another book on your shelf,

doomed to collect dust amongst all those other volumes you've wasted

money on.

And that's a shame. In a way, it would be even worse than if you'd

never read this book at all. Now that you've read this book, you can no

longer say to yourself, "I don't know how."

I have given you the HOW. If you don't take action now, you

have no one to blame but yourself.

So look at your watch. Your twenty-four-hour countdown has

begun.